I Have Something to Say

Jordan Zeitler

If you purchase this book without a cover you should be aware that this book may have been stolen property and should be reported as "unsold and destroyed" to the publisher. In such case neither the author nor the publisher has received ant payment for this "stripped book."

SECOND EDITION

Copyright © 2014 by Jordan Zeitler

All rights reserved. No part of this book may be reproduced in any form or by any electronic or mechanical means, including information storage and retrieval systems, without permission in writing from the publisher, except by a reviewer who may quote brief passages in a review.

Cover design by Lulu.com
Cover photo by Amanda Rock Photography

Jordan Zeitler
3242 Richardson Place Road, Apt #5
Arnold, MO 63010

Visit our website at
www.Lulu.com
Printed in the United States of America

This book is dedicated with love to my parents, my brother and sister, my children, and my partner, who have made this possible with their love and support.

TABLE OF CONTENTS

I. DEATH AND DYING
    Final Gift
    Going Home
    Goodbye
    Sang a Song
    Tomorrow

II. DEPRESSION
    Broken Pieces
    Can You See It in My Eyes
    Drifting
    Either Way
    The Little Boy

III. FAMILY AND FRIENDS
    Everything You Do
    I Wanna Be Like You
    More Than Words Can Say
    No One Can Compare To You
    Why I Love My Mom

IV. HUMOR
    All Lies
    Cellar Dwellers
    Drive Thru
    My Epic Tale
    Unhappily Ever After

V. LOVE
    A Prayer and A Song
    Imagine
    Something to Say
    Consequence of Not Thinking
    You Crossed the Line

VI. INSPIRATIONS AND NARRATIVES
    Century of Love
    The Dummy
    Memory Machine
    The Robot
    The Year of Roses

VII. PATRIOTISM
    A Soldier Forlorn
    Dear God
    Freedom Never Dies
    One Voice
    Soldier's Prayer

Death and Dying

The Lord is my shepherd;
I have everything I need.
He lets me rest in green meadows;
He leads me beside peaceful streams.
He renews my strength.
He guides me along right paths,
Bringing honor to his name.
Even when I walk
Through the dark valley of death,
I will not be afraid,
For you are close beside me.
Your rod and your staff
Protect and comfort me.
You prepare a feast for me
In the presence of my enemies.
You welcome me as a guest,
Anointing my head with oil.
My cup overflows with blessings.
Surely your goodness and unfailing love will pursue me
All the days of my life,
And I will live in the house of the Lord forever.
Psalms 23

I think the above verse is the perfect explanation of death. At least the best explanation of what could be. God wants to be able to welcome you to heaven with open arms. In order to get to this outcome you must live the guidelines in the bible and believe that God is the one and only. If you have done this, then your final destination will surely be one with Pearly Gates.

Thank you and enjoy the following verses.

The Final Gift

When we were young and so in love,
We held each other fast.
You promised you'd do anything
To make this feeling last.

I looked into your loving eyes
And said in words so plain,
"Just waltz with me in the kitchen
And walk with me in the rain."

The babies came, the years brought us
The stress of daily life.
We stayed together hand-in-hand,
And weathered every strife.

But when, I wondered as we watched
The years slip down the drain,
Will you waltz with me in the kitchen
And walk with me in the rain?

The children soon were grown and gone.
We held each other tight.
We laughed; we loved; we cried; we knew
That life had been all right.

But now you've gone before your time
And I live with the pain.
We'd never waltz in the kitchen;
We'd never walk in the rain.

From the deep shadows of my dreams
You came to me last night
To offer me one final gift
Before your soul took flight.

You said you couldn't travel on
Up to a higher plane
Til' you waltzed with me in the kitchen
And walked with me in the rain.

Going Home

Go rest now
Precious one,
Your life in eternity
Has just begun.

Now you can walk,
Your legs are brand new.
All of heaven
Is now in your view.

Look all around,
It's all in your sight,
There will never be
Another dark night.

Flowers and jewels,
The street of pure gold,
And all of the things
That you have been told.

I can just imagine
The smile on your face
As you walk all around
In that beautiful place.

Greeting our loved ones
As you walk along,
While singing heaven's
Most beautiful song.

This is so very hard,
But it will all be okay,
It isn't goodbye,
We'll see you one day.

We love you and we'll miss you
And at times it will be tough,
But as with everything,
God's grace will be enough.

Goodbye

You called me names,
You made me cry;
But then we changed
In the blink of an eye.

You said you were sorry
And wanted to be friends;
Who would've known
It would last till the end.

As we got older
My feelings grew;
And then you said
You loved me too.

We grew closer and closer,
More each and every day;
Nobody ever loved me
Quite the same way.

As time passed by
We laughed and smiled;
We even got married
And had a child.

As he grew older
You loved him so much;
He grew up so fast,
It was all too rushed.

Then out of the blue,
You got so sick;
I couldn't believe
It happened so quick.

One night in bed
You started to cry;
You told me you loved me,
I didn't know why.

That night God said
It was your time to go;
Why he took you from us
I'll never know.

My love for you
Will never end;
Goodbye to you,
My dearest friend.

I Sang a Song

I sang a song from deep within.
Its music was your face.
Its words sang softly your sweet voice,
And echoed sweet your grace.

Then, one day, a mournful tune.
Its music– 'twas your death.
Its words gave cause for me to weep
As you took your last breath.

They say that music's often heard
As the speech from an Angel's lips,
But I'd rather God had struck me deaf
Than lose the music of your friendship.

No longer do I hear the music played
And no longer care to listen.
I judge not God or any man
For the pain that God has given.

But if Angels are the music,
Then love's their lyrics sung.
The music for us shall long remain
And to those lyrics… I'll sing along.

But one overwhelming thought remains,
That although I loved you briefly,
You weren't just simply my music,
You were a tender symphony.

Tomorrow

Tomorrow, when you wake up,
And you see my empty chair,
I know you will feel alone,
You'll sense that I'm not there,

You'll feel I've gone, that I've moved on,
But, dear, it isn't true,
For tomorrow when you wake up,
I will still be there with you.

Tomorrow, when you make breakfast,
And you make just half as much,
Reach out with heart, with mind and soul,
And feel a tender touch,

Tomorrow when you start your day,
Please know that I am there,
For in your heart I really am,
I'm with you everywhere.

Tomorrow, when you travel through,
Your busy, tiresome day,
I'm there with you, in all you do,
As you go on your way,

Tomorrow, when you dim the light;
Then say your nightly prayers,
I will abide, there at your side
To share your worldly cares.

Someday, when you have uttered all,
Your farewells and good-byes,
When those you love stand all about
With naught but tearful eyes,

When you have crossed the threshold
That leads to eternity,
Tomorrow will be yesterday,
And you'll be here with me.

Depression

I know your probably wondering why I would put such depressing poetry in a book for everyone to read. Or write it, for that matter. Well, sadly, depression is a huge epidemic in life. No matter who you are, you have experienced a depressing moment or two. Whether it's a moment of grief because of the loss of a loved one or a chemical imbalance, you have experienced.

Now I am not a depressed person what so ever, but I have been around enough people in my life to sort of understand it. Because of their strength and ability to overcome, I am able to write these verses the way that I do.

Please read with caution. The following poems are disturbing and somewhat graphic. Also, keep in mind that no matter what frame of mind you are, be it depressed or overjoyed, God can make it better and happier as long as you believe.

The Grace Of God Will Set You Free!!

Broken Pieces

Broken pieces,
Black and blue;
His heart beats faint,
And hides the truth.
His love is fragile,
Like a rose;
It wilts away,
And no one knows.

Behind his empty smile,
Buried deep below;
Cries a long lost soul,
Not knowing where to go.
Lying in a corner,
Curled up in a ball;
He watches his world crumble,
Not knowing when he'll fall.

The dreams he has,
Is the only escape;
A place to hide,

From his lonely fate.
He's hid the pain,
Inside too long;
He had the strength,
But now it's gone.

His soul is sinking,
Deeper inside;
Below the point
Where the demons hide
He's tired of running,
And hiding his fears;
His arm swallows the blade,
And he drowns in tears.

Broken pieces,
Black and blue;
His heart beats faint,
And hides the truth.
His love is fragile,
Like a rose;
It wilts away,
And no one knows.

Can You See It In My Eyes?

You don't know how I'm feeling.
I have yet to vocalize
Desire deep inside me.
Can you see it in my eyes?

I tremble when I'm near you
Heat travels up my thighs
And I want you with an urgency
That I just can't describe.

Dare I reach out to touch you?
Do you think you'd realize
How much I want and need you?
Can you see it in my eyes?

I long to say, "I love you,"
But am scared of your reply.
Terrified like a child
I've become paralyzed.

The camouflaged emotions
Lead to pain and silent cries.
And yet I just can't tell you.
Don't you see it in my eyes?

Confessing through this poem
My dilemma summarized.
The feeling's quite cathartic,
But will lead to my demise.

Drifting

I sometimes find I'm drifting
Through this life without effect;
I often wonder if I'm truly
Worth what I've been blessed.

I search through days that have been hard,
To try to understand,
The many trials that I have known,
The life that I have had.

You see me in my daily grind,
So confident and strong;
Yet when I am alone, I question
Just where I belong.

I often try too hard I find,
To analyze and guess,
To scrutinize, investigate
My life I will confess.

For somewhere deeper, there must be
Some meaning to this life,
Some way to make a difference,
Give a reason for this strife.

Is there some hidden meaning?
Some agenda to be found?
A greater purpose waiting
If I care to hang around?

It teases and it taunts me,
Always slightly out of sight;
A hazy vision out of reach,
Where darkness hides the light.

I struggle to bring clarity
To what awaits me there,
And yet this weak illusion
Always fades before my stare.

It seems the harder that I try,
To focus through the haze,
Just serves to add more questions,
Through my endless, tired gaze.

Perhaps I'm trying just too hard,
To understand it all,
For can we ever truly know
Just what we have in store?

Each incident, each moment passed,
Just adds upon the next,
But in the end, will I find truth ...
Or will I be perplexed?

Perhaps I make it harder
then it has to be sometimes,
But will my searching bring to me
My meaning over time?

Or will it leave me broken,
And confused as I feel now,
While questions bring no solitude,
To this, my wrinkled brow.

Either Way...

Surround your heart with steel bars,
   And you shall not be pained.
   Find true love and let it fade,
     And never love again.

Alienate your heart from all,
   And it shall never break.
   Let it love, but if it's lost,
     It shall forever ache.

But keep the heart from finding love,
   And lonesomeness prevails.
   For if you close yourself to all,
     Your soul shall never sail.

Entomb your heart in walls of stone,
   And not let it be touched,
   Then never have the feeling that,
     We all long for so much.

The Little Boy

How did I get these memories?
This girl is a stranger to me
And yet I see what happened to her
I see her cry and plea

This boy was murdered by a stranger
His aura covered with fear
He screamed until his remaining breath
And his final tear

I hate to watch what happened to him
But I cannot make it stop
I know he is dead, that is for sure
In my memory I see him drop

And now his thoughts lead me here
To a place that's cold and damp
I look closer, and it is the morgue
Lit by a single lamp

The bodies are all lain out
Each one has been uncovered
He forces me to look at them
Not one is undiscovered

I look with horror at the bodies
Everyone has a story to tell
I try not to listen to the silence of the room
I force myself not to yell

This boy has brought me here for a reason
I know this for a fact
I gaze at each lifeless body
At the walls, all torn and cracked

I start to leave this horrid place
But something catches my eye
One single door has yet to be opened
He says look, and to not cry

I slowly walk to the secret door
My fear growing still
The boy tells me not to be afraid
His wishes I am to fulfill

I grab the handle and pull it open
I look at the boy, not wanting to flee
I understand why he brought me here
For that dead little boy is me

Family

What a wonderful gift, a big happy family. Although family has its ups and downs, they are your life and they love you. Family can make your most difficult situations easily repairable and they can make your happy moments even happier.

God created Eve after Adam so that they could start a family. Because of God's wisdom, we are never alone. No matter how far you are from your family, or how close, they will always be right beside you in any times of need. They will hold your hand, hug your neck, and mend your heart. So don't be afraid to lean on them.

Friendship

Just like with family, a friend will be there for you when needed. Unlike family, they are the people that you sometimes feel more comfortable with telling your deepest secrets. We live a life of necessity and friends can help take burdens and share them with you. They are people that you can count on to confide in and keep that confidential.

God should always be your best friend. He is the kind of friend that will not judge you unjustly. He is the one being that you can insure yourself in. He will not let you down; he will not let you go. He will protect you from all danger and keep your secrets safe. He will forgive and forget when you ask for it.

Everything You Do

I was sitting here thinking
Of the words I want to say,
But they just wouldn't come out right-
So I found a different way.

I got a piece of paper
And I wrote this poem for you,
But there's no way to thank you
For everything you do.

For always being nice to me
And staying by my side,
For helping fix my problems
And never leaving me behind.

For accepting my thoughts and feelings,
Though you do not understand,
For never giving up on me
And being my best friend.

For making me laugh-
And letting me cry
And saying you'd miss me
If I were to die.

Everything you mean to me
You could never know.
In all the ways you've changed my life
I could never show.

The way you take care of me,
(You're my shining star)
And though it's so incredible
That's just the way you are.

Before I get too mushy
It's time for me to go,
But before I leave this ink-filled page
There's one thing you should know.

As long as we are living,
No matter when or where,
If you ever need me-
Just call and I'll be there.

I'll climb a thousand mountains
And swim a thousand seas...
Anything to be there
'cause you've been there for me.

I Wanna Be Like You

I'd say, "Daddy, whatcha doin'?
Is there something I can do?"
"Just tell me what to do, I can do it
I wanna be like you."

"You're so big and I'm gettin' bigger-
Just give me a year or two
'Cause I'm your little man
And, if I can, I wanna be like you."

It seems like only yesterday
I saw you standin' there.
The hood was up and your hands were greasy
And there was dirt in your hair.

I know I must have been in your way
Every moment I'd spent with you.
I'll always be your little man
And I wanna be like you...

The years have passed and I've moved on
But the memories still remain
And now I have a little one
Who looks at me the same.

I heard him say the other day,
With eyes he got from you,
"I know that I'm your little man
And I wanna be like you...

I love you Dad!

More Than Words Can Say

I look back on these years
To see how far I've come and grown,
I take a trip down memory lane,
And what I see has shown ...

That every step I've taken,
You have been there by my side ...
From infancy to adulthood,
We've stood the test of time.

You cradled me and nurtured me,
Through all these many years;
You held me and did comfort me,
Through happiness and tears.

You'd pick me up when I would fall,
You'd dust me off and then,
Encourage me to get back on
That horse and ride again.

Your constant care and loving,
And your warm inviting heart,
Has always been a treasure that
I knew would n'er depart.

If I could be "just half" the person
You have been to me ...
Then you have taught me well dear mom,
For in my heart I see ...

A woman whose most gentle soul,
Embraces me each day ...
A woman whom I dearly love,
Much more than words can say.

No One Can Compare

For all those nights you didn't sleep,
And days that wouldn't end.
I thank you for being my parents,
And for being my best friends.

For all the obstacles,
You've helped me overcome,
I thank you for years of happiness,
And being a loving Mom.

For all that you've given me,
And taken from yourself,
Having you as my Father,
I have all of the world's wealth.

For all the times you took care of me,
And put your own problems on hold.
I thank you for being my Mother,
You have a heart of gold.

For all the good things you've done for me,
And things you continue to do.
I thank you for being my Father,
There's no one who can compare to you.

Why I Love My Mom

I love her 'cause she's always there,
To help me up when Life's not fair,
To kiss it better when it pains,
And scrub away the dirty stains,

To make me laugh when I am mad,
To comfort when I'm feeling sad.
And even when I'm down and blue,
She'll pick me up and push me through.

I love her 'cause she's always there,
To be my friend, to always care,
Never too busy to understand,
To love me, and to hold my hand,

To push all other things aside,
So that my needs won't be denied,
To tell me, "No," when it's not right,
To say, "Don't let the bed bugs bite."

Mom, no one can compare to you,
Without your love, what would I do?
I love you more than anyone,
I want to be just like you, Mom.

Humor

Quite simply, everyone needs a little humor in their life. I love to laugh and to make people laugh. Laughter is so important in life that I felt the need to include a few humorous verses.

ENJOY!!

All Lies

People always lie to me,
They never tell the truth.
To find out what they're telling me,
I have to be a sleuth.
My friend said he was sorry,
But I know his name is Ben,
And if my mom is in a pickle,
What am I in, then?
My dad is using Moose for Men,
My sister's eating kix.
My brother's going out tonight
To go and pick up chicks.
A frog is in my brother's throat,
Our cat is in the bag,
I'm driving mother up the wall,
This party is a drag.
My grandpa must discover
The fountain of his youth.
See? People always lie to me.
They never tell the truth.

Cellar Dwellers

How can I get my basement clean?
Those cellar dwellers are so mean!
Undoing all that I have done,
They think - perhaps I'm having fun?

Scrub as I might they do not care.
They hide in corners everywhere;
Those little fellers pink in hue
Conspirators, my work undo.

I hear them twitter at my back,
Cacophonous counter attack.
Each corner now devoid of stuff,
Upon the walls I see them stuck!!

These puny paired prolific pests
Have brand new Cellar Dweller nests.
Their young imprint me as their mom
And cling to me. Where'd they come from?

I scoop them up, neat as you please,
But - WHOOSH - they're off then with a breeze.
Sweep them again to cast them out,
"All Cellar Dwellers SCAT", I shout!!

I'll never win this war, I fear.
These Cellar Dwellers will live here
Long after this is not my home -
Pink peanut packing Styrofoam.

Drive Thru

I arose this morn with much to do -
Hopped in the car and off I flew.

No time for breakfast, that I knew -
Glad "Dunkin Donuts" has a Drive Thru.

In need of dollars, quite a few -
Went to the bank teller's Drive Thru.

Then filled all my prescriptions too -
At "Pharmacy's" brand new Drive Thru.

Some bills to mail in box of blue -
Off to the "Post Office" Drive Thru.

Picked up the laundry cleaned anew -
Just stopped at "Suds & Duds" Drive Thru.

With lunchtime near, my tummy's queue -
Got a "Big Mac" from the Drive Thru.

The car by then was low on fuel -
Full serve at "Shell", just Drive on thru.

And when they fill the tank for you -
Your cars washed free - in their Drive Thru.

Library books were overdue -
The curbside slot is a Drive Thru.

Then videos must go back too -
"Blockbuster" has their own Drive Thru.

In need of milk and bread, I knew -
I stopped at "Dairymaid's" Drive Thru.

The family asked "Please, can we do -
The "Drive In" show when dinner's thru???"

My Epic Tale

Please listen one, and listen all
To epic tale, as I recall
To weak of heart, I bid adieu
For now commence, my ode to you.

When I was six, or maybe younger
Down deep inside, I felt a hunger
To see the world, to set my sail
As to my quest, I would not fail.

I planned escape for dawn's first light
For still afraid the dark of night
With stealth I crept by parent's door
I jumped in fear, 'twas just Dad's snore.

On down the hall to living room
I did not know what terrors loom
I crouched in fear, TICK TOCK TICK TOCK
I sighed relief, just mantle's clock.

Then in search of bread and jelly
I could not leave on empty belly
O' would it cease this hunger stop?
I could not reach the countertop.

My plan awry, I forged ahead
No turning back, once left my bed
With firm resolve, I left the house
As quiet as a frightened mouse.

Across the lawn, to fence out back
Prepared to face, unknown attack
What evils lurked? I must beware
Behind the shed, in jungle there.

Amidst the leaves, I heard a sound
It was a lion! My heart did pound
With razor teeth, and claws of steel
A certain death, what pain I'd feel.

What could I do? I had no gun
My only course, turn tail and run
Back in the house and down the hall
With panting breath, on bed did fall.

Then down the hall, I heard a door
Was Mom and Dad, they slept no more
I heard Mom say, "Now what was that?"
"Oh, back doors open, it's just the cat."

My ode is over, and I must go
My tale of danger, my tale of woe
It is finished, the lesson heed
To all of you, goodbye, Godspeed.

Unhappily Ever After

As we rode off in the sunset.
Our horse threw a shoe.
Out here in the desert.
What are we to do?

After we moved in.
To our castle dear.
The door fell off, the roof caved in.
Robbing all our cheer.

Buying our new car.
Filled us with such pride.
Brakes went out, floor fell through.
I sat down and cried.

Learning how to cook.
I burnt down the house.
Angry words were said that day.
I discovered you're a louse.

Standing in the courtroom.
The judge said to me.
I will give you what you seek.
Divorce it will be.

Love & Romance

Love is patient, love is kind. It does not envy, it does not boast, it is not proud. It is not rude, it is not self-seeking, it is not easily angered, and it keeps no record of wrongs. Love does not delight in evil but rejoices with the truth. It always protects, always trusts, always hopes, and always perseveres.

Love never fails. But where there are prophecies, they will cease; where there are tongues, they will be stilled; where there is knowledge, it will pass away. For we know in part and we prophesy in part, but when perfection comes, the imperfect disappears. When I was a child, I talked like a child; I thought like a child, I reasoned like a child. When I became a man, I put childish ways behind me. Now we see but a poor reflection as in a mirror; then we shall see face to face. Now I know in part; then I shall know fully, even as I am fully known.

And now these three remain: faith, hope and love. But the greatest of these is love.

1 Corinthians 13:4-13

Love is a universal need and necessity. If you do not have love in your life, you will miss out on some of life's greatest joys. God gave us the ability to love and be loved. And by God's example, we know how to love unconditionally.

Enjoy the following verses and take the words to heart.

A Prayer and A Song

I was sort of hoping
That you'd come along.
Like the answer to a prayer,
And the music to a song

Like the kind of thing that happens
At a special place and time
That will change our lives forever,
Like a fantasy of mine.

The fantasy was there before
I even knew your name.
And now that I have found you,
We will never be the same.

So pardon if I look at you
Forgive me if I stare
At the fantasy I knew before,
I saw you standing there.

For I was always hoping,
That you would come along,
Like the answer to a prayer,
And the music to a song.

Imagine

Imagine us together
What would life be like?
We'd get up in the morning
And probably take a hike

To the hilly mountain side
Walk along a stream
Watch the cottony clouds go by
Just like in a dream

With hand in hand we would climb
Half way to the top
Then decide to take a rest
Yes, here is where we'd stop

We'd have a little picnic
Some hugs and kisses too
I'd tell you of my happiness
Since I have been with you

You'd pick some mountain flowers
Lovingly for me
And tell me how you always knew
How you and I would be

We'd probably act silly
Then head back to our nest
To cuddle and to snuggle, yes
And finally to rest

That's only to imagine but...
Just think if that were true
Wouldn't that be wonderful...?
Imagine... just me and you.

Something to Say

I said something to you today
And I know you must have heard;
I felt the answer in my heart
Although you spoke no word.

Nothing of wealth or fame,
I knew you would not mind;
I asked you to send treasures
Of a far more lasting kind.

I asked that I be near you
At the start of each new day,
To grant us smiles and happiness
And new friends to share our way.

I asked for love from you
In all things great and small,
But it was for your loving care
I asked for most of all.

The Consequence of Not Thinking

A heart's torn open,
A love is broken,
A life is empty,
With few words spoken.

The words I spoke
Aren't what they appear.
Now the loss of your love
Is the hell I fear.

You reap what you sow.
I deserve what I get.
Now I am hated.
Your mind seems to be set.

Knowing you hate me
Is a terrible fate.
I thought there was hope,
But it may be too late.

What's spoken is spoken.
And what's done is done.
I've talked without thinking,
And now you are gone.

I wish I'd shut up,
And things were the same.
I wish you didn't hurt
At the sound of my name.

But time won't go back,
And I can't make things right.
I can just say "I'm sorry"
And disappear from your sight.

You Crossed the Line

You found a way to cross the line
From dream to dream come true.
I don't know how you did it.
I don't even have a clue.

The elements you needed
Came together in a night.
It's true, every word I say.
You pulled it off just right.

A dream is sort of wishing,
Of hoping, want and such.
I felt that I was dreaming then,
I felt your hand, I felt your touch.

There was no mistake about it.
You crossed over all the way.
There you were before my eyes
And there you'll always stay.

Still, I don't know how you did it.
I don't even have a clue.
You found a way to cross the line,
And make my dreams come true.

Inspirations
&
Narrations

This small collection of poetry is very special to me. It covers a wide array of subjects. The only difference is that they are similar to short stories. These longer verses are about love, loss, and fear. Life gives us trials and tribulations that, through God, we are able to overcome. In return for us trusting in God, he gives us love and happiness. Some people search their whole life for a certain kind of happiness, others find it rather quickly. The ones who find it without trouble are the ones that trust that God will see them through.

Enjoy!!

A Century of Love

October 14, 1991

Dear Billy,
I know we're only eight years old,
But I want you to have and hold.
And every year, our love will grow,
We'll be together forever, I know.
Love, Sandy

Dear Sandy,
I thank you for the offer,
But I'm only eight years.
I can't buy you diamonds,
Or beautiful sparkling gold.
Love, Billy

Dear Billy,
Maybe someday you'll love me,
And feel the way I do.
But until that great day arrives
I'll try to wait for you.
Love, Sandy

Dear Sandy,
I can't promise we'll be together
Somewhere down the road.
I can only promise to be your friend.
Hey, I see a toad.
Love, Billy

October 14, 1996

Dear Sandy,
Now we're finally teenagers,
We're almost all grown up.
I realized that I love you
And I found out on my own.

Now may I ask a question?
Can we share our love so true,
And may I escort you to our school dance?
My suit will be dark blue.
Love, Billy

Dear Billy,
I hope this doesn't break your heart.
I hope your hurting ends.
Five years ago, I loved you so.
Now we're just best friends.

We've had so many good times.
I laugh at things we've done.
Let's just remain best friends.
That way, we'll have more fun.
Love, Sandy

October 14, 1999

Dear Billy,
I heard you your license,
And a brand new, red sports car.
Me and Johnny just broke up.
He tried to go too far.

I'm sorry if I hurt you
Three years ago today.
But in my heart, I love you so
Until my dying day.
Love, Sandy

Dear Sandy,
What are you trying to tell me?
That our love might have a chance?
I love you more and more each day,
With every passing glance.

I see in the hallway,
We hang out at the mall.
I love when we're together.
I wait for you to call.
Love, Billy

October 14, 2001

Dear Sandy,
I can't believe it's over.
Our high school years are done.
I can't wait to get to college
They say that I'll have fun.

I know we'll be apart,
But a couple years from now
I'll meet you at the church
And there, we'll exchange our vows.
Love, Billy

Dear Billy,
I wish I could start college,
But there's something you should know.
I took a test the other night,
And a little line did show.

That means I'm pregnant, Billy.
A baby's on the way.
I'm sorry if you're mad at me.
I'll make it up to you, someday.
Love, Sandy

July 14, 2002

Dear Billy,
From here on out, our lives are changed.
We'll never be the same.
This little life is ours alone
And he even has his name.

His name is Billy, Jr.
And he looks just like his dad.
I love how his eyes sparkle,
And the way he looks when he gets mad.
Love, Sandy

Dear Sandy,
What a sweet and precious little boy.
He's truly a gift from heaven.
Oh ya, I forgot to tell you,
I quit my job at the 7/11.

Don't worry about the money,
I'll make it up somehow.
I'll put in applications
Anywhere that they'll allow.
Love, Billy

October 14, 2002

Dear Sandy,
Today we join our hands and hearts.
You look gorgeous in your gown.
Our friends and family are all around.
I hope I don't fall down.

I've never been this excited.
I'm almost shedding tears.
I can't wait to say that you're my wife,
And share our happy years.
Love, Billy

Dear Billy,
I can't wait to be your wife
Forever and a day.
We'll be in love forever
In each and every way.

We'll have good times
And bad ones, too.
But at the end of each day,
We'll know we've made it through.
Love, Sandy

October 14, 2072

Dear Sandy,
It's been almost a year now,
Since the night you passed away.
Life has been so empty
With each new passing day.

Remember when we met.
We were only eight years old.
You said you had a crush on me,
But I thought you wanted gold.

I don't know if I can do this,
Keep living without you here.
I just want to be able to hold you
And wipe away your tears.

Soon I will be joining you.
I'll softly kiss your face.
I'll see you with all your beauty,
You splendor and your grace.
Love, Billy

October 14, 2083

Dear Sandy,
This will be the last time
I write you in my life.
Tonight I'm going to join you,
My precious and loving wife.

I can't believe it's been twelve years
Since I last kissed your face.
I never thought I could survive
Without you in this place.

Yesterday was my birthday.
I turned 100 years old.
I'm ready to leave this life of mine
And walk the streets of gold.

So now it's time for me to die.
I've said all my good-byes.
I'll see you in a moment, dear.
Let me dry our daughter's eyes.

Finally, we'll be together
And never be apart.
Our kids, we'll watch them night and day,
As we live within their hearts.
Love, Billy

Dear Readers,
Ten minutes after writing this,
Old Billy passed away.
In his pocket, we found these letters
That he carried every day.

They were such a good example
Of everlasting love.
They showed us love was pure of heart
And their hearts fit like hand in glove.

I can remember us just watching
Their love was amazing strong.
And since they counted on their love,
They never did go wrong.

When Grandma died,
A Part of Papa died too.
And for almost a year,
He was without a clue.

He didn't know how
He would ever survive.
Without the love of his life
There by his side.

But 12 years passed by
And Papa grew strong
Because he know he would join her
And it wouldn't take very long.

And now that their gone,
We reflect on their love.
It was perfect and pure,
A Century of Love!
Thank You, Billy III

The Dummy

In that forgotten part of town
Where wasted hopes and dreams abound,
A wrinkled man with life near end,
In hopes to have at least one friend,

Fashioned bits of wood and things
And made a dummy run by strings.
He sat alone for hours on end,
Conversing with his only friend

And found delight within the fact
That he controlled it's every act.
He told it how he never had
A chance, since all his luck was bad

Although he'd tried so to succeed -
The dummy nodded and agreed.
And how his journeys in romance
Had never given him a chance,

And wasn't it a crying shame
That he was always held to blame
When everyone knew, oh so well,
That life is but a living Hell,

Controlled by lust and power and greed?
The dummy nodded and agreed.
With patience that would rival saints,
That dummy sat through all complaints

And, with each little expert tug,
He'd droop his head or bow or shrug
And give some comfort to the man
Who held his lifelines in his hand

And helped to fill a lonely need
When he just nodded and agreed.
Senility increased with time
As did the old man's pantomime,
And feverish fingers pulled with glee
The dummy's dance of misery.

They never left each other's side
Until the day both stopped and died.
We found them laying, hand in hand,
The dummy - and his wooden friend.

The Memory Machine

Once upon a time,
As many stories start,
There was a boy and girl,
Who were worlds apart.

The girl knew the boy,
And saw him as a friend,
But the boy knew the girl,
And saw a Godsend.

She contained the essence of beauty,
She redefined that word,
But he was invisible to her,
Just one sheep among a herd.

He knew this very well,
But she still danced in his dreams,
In golden fields and meadows,
Growing by crystal streams.

One day he left,
Never to see her face,
But as fate would have it,
She left more than just a trace.

She stayed in his dreams,
Visions of her clouded his mind,
He wanted to forget,
To save himself time.

He heard of a man,
Who had a machine,
That could erase memories,
And even dreams.

He drove hundreds of miles,
Through road, dirt, and sand,
Just to see the machine,
And meet the old man.

The man's name was Charles,
His machine's name was Pearl,
And the burdened boy,
Wanted to forget the girl.

Charles asked no questions,
And made no reply,
Just gave out directions,
And watched the boy cry.

When the boy sat down,
The tubes on his head,
At the command of Charles,
Went to bed.

He dreamed once again,
Of the beautiful lass,
And as the picture faded,
He simply let it pass.

When he awoke,
He knew her no more,
And began to wonder,
Why he was on the floor.

Old man Charles,
Let the boy know,
He had let,
A memory go.

The boy asked what it was,
But Charles didn't say,
Just told him to go,
And not to pay.

So the boy left,
Wondering what was lost,
And what point in time,
It would show its true cost.

One fine morning,
He left to the store,
He was out of milk,
And needed some more.

He saw the girl,
That caused him to fret,
And when she looked back,
Their eyes met.

Something inside stirred,
But he ignored the sting,
And his body told him,
Forgetting was a bad thing.

He looked a little longer,
And remembered,
He remembered...
Nothing.

And the girl walked away,
Tossing the meeting behind,
And the boy suppressed hurt,
He thought was only in his mind.

The Robot

Upon the stairway of despair,
Complete with broken love affairs
And promises that never came,
But faded with a touch of shame,

A pretty girl with golden hair
And innocence so sadly rare,
Strove to keep her head above
A way of life devoid of love.

Feeling pinned against Life's wall,
She chanced upon a robot tall
And said, "Please come and share with me
Whatever Fate has deemed to be.

I'm through with love, done with chances
Spirit crushed by past romances,
Just be a friend in word and deed.
That's all that I shall ever need."

"There's not too much from me to learn,"
Remarked the robot, in return.
"Emotions do not form a part
of my cold, solid-steel heart.

Whatever maker fashioned me
Did not permit my circuitry
Responsiveness to love or pain -
You're thoughts for me would be in vain."

"No matter", spoke the maid. "No more
Do I wish passion to explore.
Be someone I can come home to
When my exhausting day is through.

Count yourself a well-worn shoe -
A friend that I can slip into . . .
Protection from a stone cold floor . . .
For this I ask and nothing more."

Agreement made, he took her hand
And lived the life that she had planned,
Always willing, not demanding,
Aiding her with understanding

He made her smile with humorous wit
(As his restrictions would permit)
And, bit by bit, she came to feel
That he was more than iron and steel.

"I love you, robot", she at last
Replied when several months had passed.
"You're strength and quiet dignity
Have brought a wondrous change in me.

No more do I feel all alone,
And pray you must be flesh and bone.
Deep-set emotions you MUST feel
Within that outer coat of steel!"

"If I were able, I would say
I'm sorry I was made this way
But my design and programmation
Does not provide for that creation

Of feelings normal men may feel
That were not born of iron and steel.
I told you all this once before.
You have no right expecting more."

"Go, then!" cried she. "I will not live
Beside a friend who cannot give!
Though I be battered by misuse,
Misguided trust and strong abuse,

At least the men I chose were real
And had the power to love and feel.
Of all the lovers I recall,
You are the cruelest one of all!"

The robot, indestructible,
Continues freely and at will.
Emotionless, apparently,
But, bearing closer scrutiny,

One can see a small tear streak
Down that cold, metallic cheek
As I reflect upon my life . . .
That lovely lady was my wife.

The robot, of course, was me.

The Year of Roses

Each year he sent her roses,
and the note would always say,
I love you even more this year,
than last year on this day.

My love for you will always grow,
with every passing year.
She knew this was the last time
that the roses would appear.

She thought, he ordered roses
in advance before this day.
Her loving husband did not know,
that he would pass away.

He always liked to do things early,
way before the time.
Then, if he got too busy,
everything would work out fine.

She trimmed the stems and placed them,
in a very special vase.
Then, sat the vase beside
the portrait of his smiling face.

She would sit for hours,
In her husband's favorite chair.
While staring at his picture,
and the roses sitting there.

A year went by, and it was
to live without her mate.
With loneliness and solitude,
that had become her fate.

Then, the very hour struck,
and not one minute more.
The doorbell rang, and there were,
roses sitting by her door.

She brought the roses in,
and then just looked at them in shock.
Then, went to get the telephone,
to call the florist shop.

The owner answered, and she asked him,
if he would explain,
Why would someone do this to her,
causing her such pain?

I know your husband passed away,
more than a year ago,
The owner said, I knew you'd call,
and you would want to know.

The flowers you received today,
were paid for in advance.
Your husband always planned ahead,
he left nothing to chance.

There is a standing order,
that I have on file down here,
And he has paid, well in advance,
you'll get them every year.

There also is another thing,
that I think you should know,
He wrote a special little card,
he did this years ago.

Then, should ever I find out
that he's no longer here,
that's the card that should be sent
to you the following year.

She thanked him and hung up the phone,
her tears now flowing hard.
Her fingers shaking, as she slowly
reached to get the card.

Inside the card, she saw that he
had written her a note.
Then, as she stared in total silence,
this is what he wrote...

Hello my love, I know it's been
a year since I've been gone.
I hope it hasn't been too hard
for you to overcome.

I know it must be lonely,
and the pain is very real.
Or if it was the other way,
I know how I would feel.

The love we shared made everything
so beautiful in life.
I loved you more than words can say,
you were the perfect wife.

You were my friend and lover,
you fulfilled my every need.
I know it's only been a year,
but please try not to grieve.

I want you to be happy,
even when you shed your tears.
That is why the roses will be
sent to you for years.

When you get these roses,
think of all the happiness
that we had together,
and how both of us were blessed.

I have always loved you
and I know I always will.
But, my love, you must go on,
you have some living still.

Please...try to find happiness,
while living out your days.
I know it is not easy,
but I hope you find some ways.

The roses will come every year,
and they will only stop,
When your door's not answered,
when the florist stops to knock.

He will come five times that day,
in case you have gone out.
But after his last visit,
he will know without a doubt!

To take the roses to the place,
where I've instructed him
and place the roses where we are,
together once again.

Patriotism

As a member of the Armed Services, I have a whole new respect for patriotism. I grew up thinking that I would never join the military, but since I have, I have seen things that I would have never seen otherwise. I have been to numerous countries and experienced the pride of knowing that what I do every day saves the lives of the soldiers fighting overseas for the freedom we so take advantage of.

God Bless America. That is a phrase that is so unappreciated. Because of the separation of church and state, that phrase is no longer important to the people of America. It was taken from our pledge of allegiance and our money. Our country was built on morals and values that were established by the Bible and the word of God.
But we have begun to lose those values. As a serviceman, I am a protector of our country. I may not fight in battle or even carry a gun, but what I do every day is essential to the freedom of our country.

With that in mind, also keep this in mind. I am a soldier of the United State of America. I am a soldier of Jesus Christ. The Lord of Lords, The Alpha and The Omega, The Beginning and The End. It is his orders that I follow daily because without his orders, I would be nothing.

So God Bless America!!

A Soldier Forlorn

A returning soldier walks the road,
Armed with his musket, sword and fife,
His eyes proud gleam boasts his life,

An ivory mane crowns his head held high,
With silver buttons and a crisp waistcoat,
Entrances women, who giggle and dote,

They see his silhouette on the setting sun,
Regard his stature and arrogant visage,
As if his potent bearing is a mirage,

Eyes fixed ahead on the dusty path,
For they do not see the scars of battle,
Underneath his decorated, valiant apparel,

Memory harkens beneath his façade,
A fresh faced youth headed his platoon,
Thousands of marching figures upon high noon,

Returning to the pathway a weary warrior,
His heart slowly scorched to stone,
Hardened by the abhorrence it did hone,

As he strides along the dusty road,
Recollection haunts his route,
Vividly, replaying is the horror astute,

A faceless enemy lurks from afar,
Hail of bullets falling from the pits of hell,
Comrades falling, like angels they dwell,

Blood slowly soaked into the swampish loam,
Reminiscent crimson blotches all but remain,
As he tries to rid his conscious of wounding blame,

The screams echoed in the humid vegetation,
The smell of fear and blood hung in the air,
As another was hit, another lost prayer,

Gallantly they were told the battle was won,
But the images death, raging in is head,
Tell of a different story, an ulterior end,

A returning soldier walks the road,
His dauntless figure swanks his deeds,
While deep inside, his soul bleeds.

Dear God

Dear God, I want to say,
A special prayer in a special way.
May you bless those far and near
Brighten a smile and dry a tear.

Who could forget that terrible day
America was attacked in a horrific way?
God, please show them that you're near.
Touch a soul to show you care.

Guide them every day and night
Let them know they'll be all right.
Help them to heal day by day
And show them they're loved in every way.

Bless people far and near
Who helped out others and showed they cared.
Bless those who passed away
For their love will never stray.

God, I know you'll hear my prayer
And you'll bless everyone everywhere.
Please take our pain away.
God, please bless the U.S.A

Freedom Never Dies

September eleventh, two thousand and one,
The whole world got to see
The towering twins of New York City
Fall so helplessly.

They both were struck by suicide jets
On a mission to destroy
The spirit of America
And the freedoms we enjoy.

Then a third jet struck our Pentagon
While a fourth jet couldn't go
Beyond the Pennsylvania trees
Cause of heroes we now know.

So with vengeance left to be the Lord's
One thing still applies.
Freedom just might cost your life,
But freedom never dies.

One Voice

I've tried to find the words today
To tell what's in my heart,
A way to vent… a way to share
But how is one to start?

How do we write the horror
Of the thousands who were lost?
How do we pen the terror felt
As lives became the cost?

How do we say "Good will prevail -
We shall not be defeated."
How do we shout with confidence
"Such acts won't be repeated!"

How do we quell the anger
Reaching far beyond the brink?
How do we spill the endless tears
That flow in crimson ink?

How do we rise up full of pride
In silent rage no longer?
Together, my friends… we must be heard
One voice… united… stronger!

A Soldier's Prayer

It's time to sleep
I've been relieved
My rifle at my side
My knife in its sheath

Lord let me live another day
As I put myself in harm's way
I made my choice, I took the oath
I stand for freedom, but I don't boast

My God, my country, my family
The things I hold so dear
With these all on my side
There's nothing for me to fear

But if I should fall before my next relief
I will stand before you Lord with honor and dignity
So, while I'm here please make me strong
To fight the battles and right what's wrong

A Confetti of

PAPERS